Add a teddy bear and blocks to a photo of a sweet baby girl for an announcement of love.

It's a Girl!
Design Originals 'Little Baby Faces' paper • Cardstock (Mauve, Pale Pink, Pale Green, Green fleck, Lavender, Yellow, Black) • Pink 'It's A Girl' die cut • $5/8$" Black letter stickers • 2 Pink eyelets • 1" Pink tassel • Pink cotton crochet thread • Pop-Dots • Black pen • Jumbo Scallop scissors • Circle punches ($1/8$" eyes, $1/2$" ears, $3/4$" ears, 2" body and head) • Heart punches ($3/8$" nose, $3/4$" muzzle, 2" arms and legs) • $15/16$" square punch for the blocks

Baby Card & Envelope
Design Originals 'Little Baby Faces' paper • Cardstock (Pink, Pale Pink, Pale Green, Green fleck, Lavender, Yellow, White, Black) • $5/8$" Black letter stickers • 2 Pink eyelets • 1" Pink tassel • Pink cotton crochet thread • Pop-Dots • Black pen • Jumbo Scallop scissors • Circle punches ($1/8$" eyes, $1/2$" ears, $3/4$" ears, 2" body and head) • Heart punches ($3/8$" nose, $3/4$" muzzle, 2" arms and legs) • $15/16$" square punch for block

Cards - Score and fold a piece of $5½$" x $8½$" cardstock to make a $4¼$" x $5½$" card. Cut with wavy edge scissors to make a decorative border.

Pull the Tassel to Make the Bear Move!

For a 'moving' statement, add a Jumping Jacks teddy to your birth announcement.

Bear Body Pattern

Bear Arm Pattern

Bear Face Pattern

See envelope pattern on page 8.

To make Bear move, see page 9 "How to Thread".

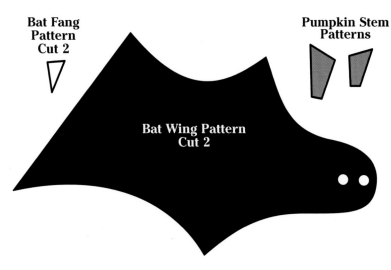

Pull the Tassel to Make the Animal Move!

Cut Here for Card

Jumping Jacks

Make Moveable Pages Fun!

Bat Head/Body Pattern

Bat Fang Pattern Cut 2

Pumpkin Stem Patterns

Bat Wing Pattern Cut 2

Tree Trunk Pattern

A bat flaps his wings and jack-'o-lanterns grin… it's time to gather the gang and 'Trick or Treat'.

Trick or Treat Bat

Design Originals 'Orange Cobwebs' paper • Cardstock (Orange, Black, White, Lime Green, Brown fleck) • ⅝" Black letter stickers • 2 Black eyelets • 1" Black tassel • Black cotton crochet thread • Pop-Dots • Black pen • Scallop scissors • Punches (½" heart bat ears and feet, ⅝" maple leaf, ⅝" spiral) • Circle punches (⅛" bat eyes, ¼" bat nose, 1" pumpkin, 1¼" pumpkin, 1¾" bat head)

To make Bat move, see page 9 "How to Thread".

Tree Top Pattern

Banana Pattern

Monkey Face Pattern

Cut here & below for card.

A TRIP TO THE ZOO WITH GRAM

A favorite at the zoo is a visit to the monkeys. Hang a moveable monkey in a tree to bring back memories.

A Trip to the Zoo
Cardstock (Rust fleck, Tan, White, Black, Yellow, Lime Green, Brown Craft) • AccuCut Green grass die cut • ⅝" Green letter stickers • 2 Tan eyelets • 1" White tassel • White cotton crochet thread • Pop-Dots • Brown marker • Black pen • Deckle scissors • Circle punches (⅛" eyes, ¼" eyes and ears, ⁵⁄₁₆" nose, eyes and ears, 1" head and face, 1⅝" body)

To make Monkey move, see page 9 "How to Thread".

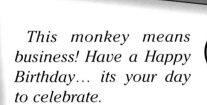

This monkey means business! Have a Happy Birthday… its your day to celebrate.

Birthday Card & Envelope
Provo 'Rust check' paper • Cardstock (Tan marble, Rust, Tan, White, Black, Yellow, Lime Green, Brown craft) • ½" Green letter stickers • 2 Tan eyelets • 1" White tassel • White cotton crochet thread • Pop-Dots • Black pen • Deckle scissors • Circle punches (⅛" eyes, ¼" nose, eyes and ears, ⁵⁄₁₆" eyes and ears, 1" head and face, 1⅝" body)

See envelope pattern on page 8.

Monkey Arm & Leg Pattern

Monkey Body Pattern

Jumping Jacks

Face Pattern

Gingerbread Arm Pattern Cut 2

Gingerbread Body Pattern

Gingerbread Leg Pattern Cut 2

Fill Holiday memories with scents of homemade goodies from the kitchen.

Gingerbread Man

Design Originals 'Green stripe' paper • Cardstock (Green, White, Red, Dark Red, Golden Brown) • ⅝" Red letter stickers • 4 Tan eyelets • 1" Red tassel • Red cotton crochet thread • Pop-Dots • Red and Black pens • Corkscrew scissors • Wavy edge ruler • Circle punches (1" peppermint, 1¼" head) • Heart punches (¼" cheeks, ⅜" buttons)
TIP: Use ruler to make wavy border.

Pull the Tassel to Make the Gingerbread Man Move!

Candy Cane Pattern

To make the Gingerbread Man move, see page 9 "How to Thread".

A fat little gingerbread man dances a holiday greeting on this delicious card.

Peppermint Pattern

Holiday Card & Envelope

Design Originals 'Green stripe' paper • Cardstock (Green, White, Red, Dark Red, Golden Brown) • ½" Red letter stickers • 4 Tan eyelets • 1" Red tassel • Red cotton crochet thread • Pop-Dots • Red and Black pens • Corkscrew scissors • 1¼" circle punch for head • Heart punches (¼" cheeks, ⅜" buttons)
See envelope pattern on page 8.

Santa Hat Pattern

Santa Leg & Sleeve Trim Cut 4

Santa Mustache Pattern

Santa Hat Trim

Santa Body Pattern

Santa Arm Pattern Cut 2

Santa Hat Trim Pattern

JINGLE BELLS

Pull Tassel to See Santa Move!

Gifts and Santa…
The tree is piled high
with packages and the house jingles with joy.

Santa Claus

Design Originals paper ('Music Melody', 'Red stripe', 'Red dot', 'Green check', 'Green heart') • Cardstock (Deep Red, Green, White, Black, Flesh) • ⅝" Black letter stickers • 2 Red eyelets • 1" Red tassel • Red cotton crochet thread • Pop-Dots • Pink chalk • Black pen • Mini Scallop and Deckle scissors • Circle punches (⁵⁄₁₆" bow, nose and mouth, ⅝" hat trim, 2" head) • Heart punches (⅜" bow, ¾" bow, 2" beard, mustache and boot)

Gift Box Sizes - 1⅛" x 1½", 1½" x 1⅞", 2¼" x 2¼"

To make Santa move, see page 9 "How to Thread".

Santa Hand Pattern Cut 2

Santa Legs Pattern

*These little angels love to play in the sand.
And for now, their halos are shining brightly.*

Our Little Angels

Design Originals 'Blue Gingham' paper • Cardstock (Blue, Yellow, White, Flesh) • Vellum • 4 White eyelets • 2 White 1" tassels • White cotton crochet thread • Pop-Dots • Blue pen • Stylus • Cardboard • Scallop and Corkscrew scissors • Punches (1¼" circle halo, ¾" heart hands and feet)
TIPS: Use a computer to print the title and color with a pen. Place pattern on cardboard. Place vellum face down on pattern and emboss with stylus.

Envelopes - Lightly trace pattern on cardstock. Score fold lines. Fold side flaps. Fold bottom flap up and glue to sides. For variations, use printed paper with White side out or print paper glued to solid color cardstock.

Envelope Pattern

Fold

Fold

Fold

Fold

Pull the Tassel to Move the Wings!

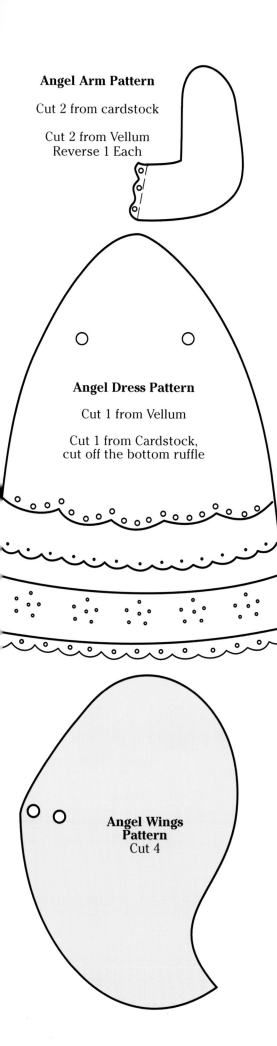

Angel Arm Pattern

Cut 2 from cardstock

Cut 2 from Vellum
Reverse 1 Each

Angel Dress Pattern

Cut 1 from Vellum

Cut 1 from Cardstock,
cut off the bottom ruffle

**Angel Wings
Pattern**
Cut 4

Jumping Jacks

Make characters with arms and legs that move... simply attach eyelets, add thread and a tassel or bead. Pull for movement. Hold the page vertically and the moving parts return to their original position. It's so easy!

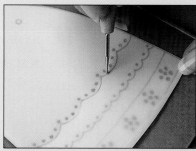

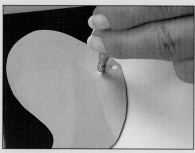

1. Cut all pattern pieces from cardstock. For angel, place dress pattern on cardboard. Place Vellum right side down on pattern and emboss (trace over lines) with a stylus. Cut out the dress.

2. Set eyelets required for design. Legs, arms and wings require two ⅛" punched holes.

The eyelet is inserted in the inside hole.

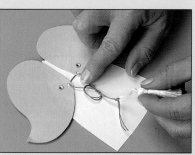

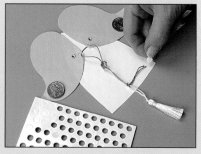

3. Thread 12" of cotton crochet thread through outside holes. Bring thread ends together and tie an Overhand knot about 1" below punched holes.

Overhand Knot

4. Thread a tassel or bead on one thread end. Bring thread ends together and tie an Overhand knot to secure.

Be sure thread will not show below bottom of design when tassel is pulled down.

Glue pennies or washers to end of legs, arms or wings. Hold page upright... when tassel is pulled the weight will bring piece back to its original position.

TIP

Attach design to prepared album page with Pop-Dots. Place dots only on sections that do not move. Be sure they are positioned so that arms, legs or wings can move freely.

Moveable Kids

Playgrounds are the places where precious childhood memories are made… from swings to teeter-totters to sandboxes.

Play Time

Design Originals 'Red plaid' and 'Red dot' paper • Pale Blue paper • Robin's Nest Denim paper • Cardstock (Olive Green, Red, Tan fleck, Flesh, Brown, Golden Brown, Yellow, Golden Yellow) • ⅝" Red letter stickers • Tan eyelet • Pens (Black, Red, Brown) • Pink chalk • Scissors (Jumbo Deckle, Deckle, Stamp, Pinking) • Circle punches (¼" ears, ⅝" spinner base, 1" face, hair and headband, 1¼" hair, 1⅝" sun face, 2" sun rays)

See 'Play Time' patterns on page 13.

Overalls and a tricycle… comfortable clothes and a favorite mode of transportation make a wonderful day.

Tricycle

Provo 'Green Grass' paper • Robin's Nest 'Denim' paper • Cardstock (Orange, Blue, Royal Blue, Brown, Black, Gray, Flesh) • ⅝" Blue letter stickers • 2 Blue and 5 Black eyelets • Black and Red pens • Pink chalk • Stamp scissors • ¾" heart punch for shoe • Circle punches (⅛" cap button, ¼" ears, ¾" cap brim and wheels, 1" head, cap and spinner base, 1¼" wheels, 1½" wheel, 2" wheel) • ½" square punch for pedal

TIPS: Front wheel is 1½" Gray, 2" Black and 1" spinner base circles. Do not glue leg to page. Turn front wheel with finger to make the boy pedal the tricycle.

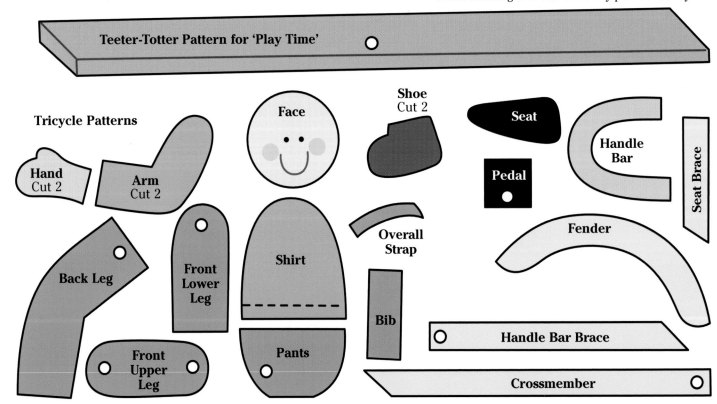

Teeter-Totter Pattern for 'Play Time'

Tricycle Patterns

Hand
Cut 2

Arm
Cut 2

Face

Shoe
Cut 2

Seat

Pedal

Handle Bar

Seat Brace

Back Leg

Front Lower Leg

Shirt

Overall Strap

Fender

Front Upper Leg

Pants

Bib

Handle Bar Brace

Crossmember

Eyelets Give Kids Mobility on Pages!

Suzy-Q's an athlete that can move on your page. Put her on a scooter and let her fly with the wind.

Suzy-Q on a Scooter

Carolee's Creations 'Blue Weave' paper • Sonburn 'Blue Daisy' paper • Cardstock (White, Yellow textured, Blue, Golden Brown, Flesh, Black, Tan fleck) • Chubby letter stencil • Eyelets (Yellow, White, 2 Black) • Black and Red pens • Pink chalk • Scallop and Corkscrew scissors • 1" daisy punch • Circle punches (¼" daisy center, ¾" wheels, 1" face, hair and headband, 1½" hair)

TIP: Glue only scooter base, wheels and front leg to page. Glue back arm to scooter handle. Do not glue back arm to dress.

Backyard Fun

Summer days mean backyard fun. Swinging, sliding and enjoying the sun.

Backyard Fun
Design Originals 'Sky & Clouds' paper • Cardstock (Flesh, Golden Brown, Deep Red, Blue, Tan fleck, Brown, Green) • Green grass die cut • $5/8$" Red dot letter stickers • Silver eyelet • Pop Dots • Black and Red pens • Pink chalk • Deckle and Scallop scissors • Circle punches ($1/4$" ears, 1" face, hair and spinner base, $1\frac{1}{4}$" spinner base) • $3/4$" heart punch for shoes
Swing Ropes -Cut two $1/8$" x 8" rectangles from Tan cardstock

Eyelets give this Swing Mobility!

Face

Hand
Cut 2

Arm
Cut 2

Shirt

Leg

Pants

Leg

Swing Seat

Tree Top

Cut one long & one short piece along dashed line.

Tree Trunk

Easy Eyelets are a fantastic way to give your pages that extra pizzazz!

Play Time Patterns
Continued from page 10.

Face
Cut 2

Sleeve
Cut 2

Sun Face

Shirt
Cut 2

Arm
Cut 2

Handle
Cut 2

Shorts
Cut 2

Leg
Cut 2

Note:
Teeter-Totter Pattern on page 10.

Teeter-Totter Leg - Cut 2

Moveable Kids

Spinner bases allow you to make swings, wheels and even a teeter-tooter move.

1. Cut and punch all pattern pieces. Punch ⅛" holes as marked. If design calls for a spinner base, cut the required circle or circles, punch a ⅛" hole at center and attach to back of pattern piece with eyelet.

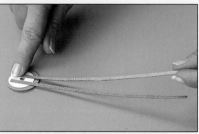

2. To make swing, cut two ⅛" x 8" strips. Glue strips to 1" circle for ropes. For other designs, match ⅛" holes and join pieces with eyelets. Set eyelets firmly. Glue remaining pattern pieces together.

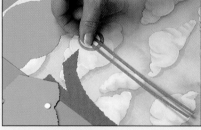

3. Glue spinner base or stationary sections to prepared album page.

4. For swing, attach Pop-Dots to back of large Green tree section. Place over spinner base and ropes.

Broom Stick

Witch Broom

Cloud Pattern

Bat Ears

Face

Hat Star

Hat Band

Hat Brim

Leg

A witch spins through the sky revealing photos of Happy Halloween fun.

Flying Witch

Design Originals 'Purple stripe' paper, Cardstock (Deep Blue, Yellow, Black, Purple, Lime Green, Orange, Brown, Tan, White, Gray marble) • Yellow eyelet • Pop-Dots • Black pen • Black chalk • Scallop, Deckle & Stamp wavy scissors • Circle punches ($\frac{1}{2}$" bat body, $\frac{3}{4}$" witch face, witch bangs and bat wings, 1" witch hair) • Heart punches ($\frac{3}{4}$" foot and hand, $1\frac{1}{4}$" witch arm and hat, 2" witch body and skirt) • Punches ($1\frac{1}{8}$" cat, $\frac{1}{4}$" star, $\frac{1}{2}$" star)
TIP: Cut a $7\frac{3}{8}$" spinner wheel.

Ghost Pattern

Spinner Wheels

Reveal Hidden Photos to Make Pages Fun!

Bed
Knob
Cut 2

Heart

Bed

Count the sheep, spin the wheel and reveal a cherished photo.

Counting Sheep

Blue flower paper • Cardstock (Tan parchment, Wedgwood Blue, White, Black) • ⅝" White letter stickers • Blue eyelet • Pop Dots • Blue pen • Scissors (Stamp, Scallop, Jumbo Scallop) • Punches (1" circle bedpost, ¾" heart sheep leg and face, 1¼" heart bed)
TIP: Cut a 6¼" spinner wheel.

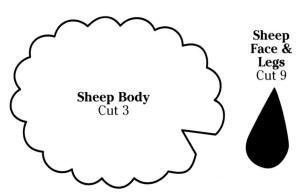

Sheep Body
Cut 3

Sheep
Face &
Legs
Cut 9

Fold

Turn the Wheel to Make the Sheep Move and Reveal the Baby!

Spinner Wheels
Make Pages Fun!

A tiny train chugs around a circle carrying a load of love and memories.

Chug-Chug, Toot-Toot
Design Originals 'Stepping Stones' paper • Bo Bunny 'Press Pale Green' paper • Cardstock (White, Deep Red, Blue, Black, Yellow) • Red ⅝" letter stickers • One Green and 12 Black eyelets • Stamp scissors • Circle punches (⅝" wheels, ¾" wheels) • ⅝" cloud punch for smoke
TIP: Cut a 6¼" spinner wheel. Cut 3½" Black circle track and a 3" Green center circle with stamp scissors.

Chug-Chug   Toot-Toot

Turn the 'Spinner Wheel' to Move the Train and Reveal the Photos!

Top for Train Caboose

Train Car & Photo Block
Cut 3

Smoke

Smoke Stack

Top for Engine Cab

Cattle Catcher for front of Engine

Bee Head

Bee Body

Beehive

Turn the Wheel to Make the Bumble Bees Move and Reveal the Photos!

Make yard work a family activity and your hive will be filled with happy times.

Busy Bees

Design Originals 'Garden Leaves' paper • Cardstock (Olive Green, Yellow, Black, Tan textured, Brown) • Vellum • ⅝" Black letter stickers • Pop Dots • Pens (Black, Brown, White) • Punches (¾" circle head, 1¼" heart wings, ⅝" spiral legs and antennae)
TIP: Cut a 5½" spinner wheel.

Turn the 'Spinner Wheel' to Make the Frogs Move and Reveal the Photos!

Frog Face Pattern

Dragonfly Wing Patterns

Dragonfly Head Pattern

Cattail Patterns

Dragonfly Body Pattern

Toadally Awesome Kid!

Every kid is a real treasure... but your special ones are 'toad-ally' awesome.

'Toad-ally' Awesome Kid
Design Originals 'Stepping Stones' paper • Cardstock (Spring Green, Pale Green, White, Red, Black, Baby Blue, Medium Blue, Rust) • Red ⅝" letter stickers • Blue eyelet • Pop-Dots • Black and Red pens • Scallop scissors • Punches (⅜" heart for cheeks, ⅝" spiral for dragonfly antennae) • Circle punches (¼" toad eyes, ⁵⁄₁₆" dragonfly head, ½" toad eyes, ¾" toad eyes and feet)
TIP: Cut a 6" spinner wheel.

Spinner Wheels

Attach photos and shapes to a 'Spinning Wheel'. Then spin the wheel for exciting photos and pages.

1. Cut the required size of wheel from cardstock. If necessary, cover the wheel with a patterned paper to match the background paper. Cut 3" cardstock circle. Punch ⅛" hole at center of both circles. Place 3" circle on back of wheel matching ⅛" holes. Attach 2 circles by setting an eyelet through holes.

Turn the 'Wheel' to Move the Sun and Reveal the Photos!

Friends and a walk in the park make a rainbow of happy memories to be recalled with this sunshine page.

Sunny Day

Design Originals 'Blue Clouds' paper • Cardstock (Red, Yellow, Blue, White, Light Orange, Bright Orange) • ⅝" Red dot letter stickers • White eyelet • Pop-Dots • Black and Red pens • Corkscrew scissors • Punches (2" circle sun, ⅝₁₆" heart cheeks)

TIP: Cut Red 7⅜", Yellow 6", Blue 4¼" and cloud paper 2¾" circles.

Use Cloud pattern on page 14

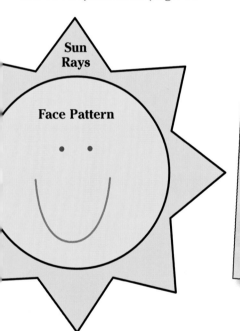

Sun Rays

Face Pattern

2. Glue 3" circle to prepared album page. Spinner wheel should turn easily. Decorate wheel.

3. Cut design element that will cover the lower half of wheel. Apply Pop Dots to back.

4. Attach design element to page placing it over bottom half of wheel and just barely covering eyelet in center of wheel. Complete page with title and photos.

A Time
For Us

Move the Clock Hands to
Record the Memory of
that Special Time!

Poseable Shapes

Take time to create special loving memories and record them on a timeless page.

A Time for Us

Keeping Memories Alive Brown wool plaid paper • Cardstock (Brown, Metallic Gold, Cream parchment) • 3/8" Metallic Gold number stickers • 2 Gold eyelets • Brown pen • Scallop scissors • 3/4" circle punch for pendulum

TIP: Cut 3⅞" Metallic Gold circle, 3¾" Cream parchment circle. Cut 1¹⁵/₁₆" x 2¹/₁₆" Brown cardstock for Back of Pendulum Case. Print page title on computer and color letters.

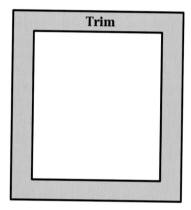

Trim

Clock Base

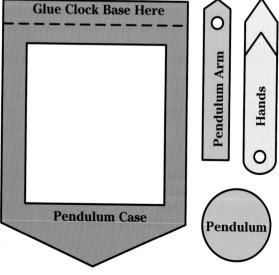

Glue Clock Base Here

Pendulum Case

Pendulum Arm

Hands

Pendulum

Even friends who have never sewn a stitch would love to receive this heartfelt greeting card.

Love Card & Envelope

Red dot paper • Cardstock (Light Blue parchment, Deep Red, Blue, Tan marble) • Red embroidery floss • Blue eyelet • Scallop scissors • 1/8" circle punch
TIP: Print words on computer.

See envelope pattern on page 8.

Love is truly an unending, unbreakable thread that binds families and friends.

Love is the Thread

Design Originals Heritage Quilt paper • Cardstock (White, Deep Red, Blue, Tan marble) • Light Gold braided cord • Blue eyelet • Scallop and Jumbo Scallop scissors • 1/8" circle punch
TIP: Print words on computer.

Hearts
Cut 1 each

Fold

Needle

Spool for Card

Scissors
Cut 2

Spool for Page

Love is the thread that binds all hearts together

This invitation will move your guests to anticipate an evening of Halloween fun.

Halloween Party Invitation & Envelope
Pixie Press 'Black Moon and Stars' paper • Cardstock (Orange, White, Brown, Olive Green, Black) • ½" White letter stickers • 4 White eyelets • Black pen • Zig Zag scissors • Circle punches (¼" eyes, 2" pumpkins, 1¼" maple leaf, ⅝" spiral)
TIP: Fill in around ribs with Black pen.

See envelope pattern on page 8.

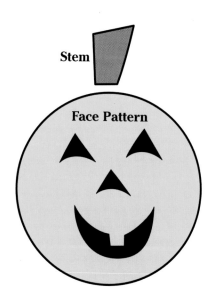

Stem

Face Pattern

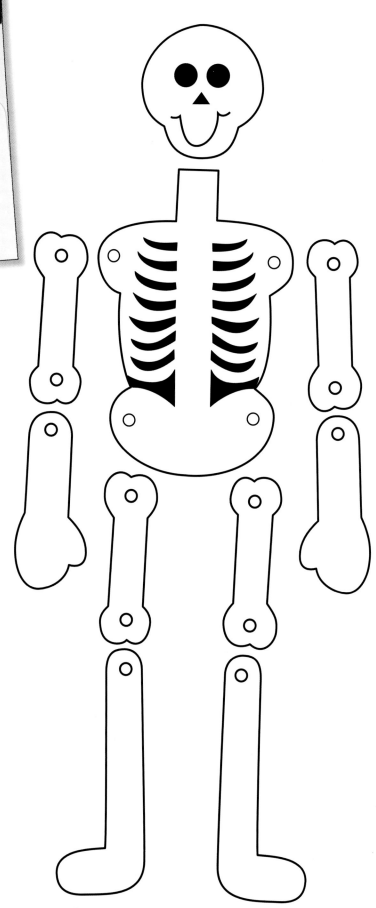

Move the Skeleton's Arms and Legs to Create a Friendly Pose!

This cute Halloween page features an even cuter little clown.

Halloween Skeleton

Design Originals 'Gold Stars on Navy' paper • Cardstock (Orange, White) • Orange Halloween die cut • 8 White eyelets • Black pen • Zig Zag scissors • ¼" circle punch for eyes

TIP: Fill around ribs with a Black pen.

Poseable Shapes

Bring Fun to Album Pages!

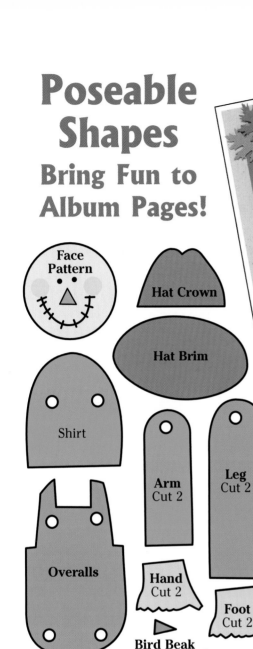

Face Pattern

Hat Crown

Hat Brim

Shirt

Arm Cut 2

Leg Cut 2

Overalls

Hand Cut 2

Foot Cut 2

Bird Beak

Pumpkin Stem Cut 3

Give Thanks

Pumpkin patches, scarecrows and falling leaves… a sure sign that fall is here.

Fall Leaves

Karen Foster Design Ginger paper • Robin's Nest Press Blue Denim paper • Design Originals Red plaid paper • Cardstock (Brown, Olive Green, Yellow textured, Yellow, Orange, Dark Rust, Light Rust, Black, Tan fleck, Gold) • 2 Red and 2 Blue eyelets • Red and Black pens • White gel pen • Pink chalk • Deckle scissors • Chubby 1½" letter stencil • Punches (1¼" oak leaf, ⁷⁄₁₆" heart crow wing, ¾" heart crow body) • Circle punches (⁵⁄₁₆" crow head, 1" face, hair and pumpkins, 1¼" pumpkins)
TIP: Cut Scarecrow stand strips from Tan fleck ¼" x 3" and ¼" x 4½".

A friendly scarecrow invites you to give thanks and celebrate autumn.

'Give Thanks' Card & Envelope

Robin's Nest Press 'Blue Denim' paper • Design Originals 'Red plaid' and 'Fall Acorns & Leaves' paper • Cardstock (Ivory parchment, Brown, Yellow textured, Yellow, Rust, Orange, Olive Green, Gold, Flesh, Black) • ½" Red letter stickers • 2 Red and 2 Blue eyelets • Black and Red pens • White gel pen • Pink chalk • Deckle scissors • Circle punches (⁵⁄₁₆" crow head, 1" head and hair) • Punches (1¼"oak leaf, ⁷⁄₁₆" heart crow wing, ¾" heart crow body)

See envelope pattern on page 8.

Let us be thankful for the family, the feast and the fun.

Head

Beak

Fold

Buckle

Wattle

Hatband

Hat Brim

Outer Tail

Inner Tail

Turkey

Design Originals 'Gold stripe' paper • Cardstock (Orange, Light Orange, Brown fleck, Black, Deep Red, White, Yellow) • 3 Tan eyelets • Brown pen • Cloud scissors • Circle punches (1/8" eyes, 1/4" buckle) • 5/8" square for buckle

TIP: Cut 2¾" Brown fleck circle for body. Print the title on computer and color letters with pen.

Let Us Be Thankful

Move the Turkey's Head and Wings to Change his Pose!

Wing
Cut 2

Foot
Cut 2

Hat Crown

Poseable Shapes

Can Make Animals Rock and Fly!

Move the Chicken's Wings and Legs to a Fun and Entertaining Pose!

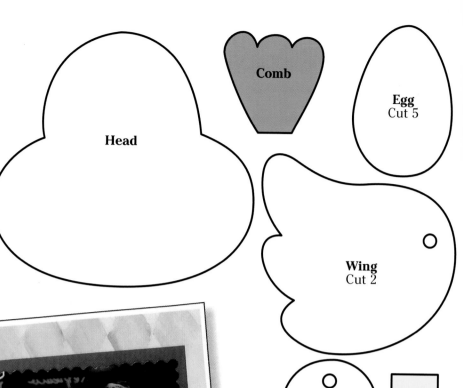

A proud mama and her little chick grace a page with love and happy memories.

Little Chick

Design Originals 'Heritage Diamonds' paper • Cardstock (White, Deep Red, Yellow, Black, Brown craft) • 5/8" Red letter stickers • 4 White eyelets • Scallop scissors • Punches (1/4" circle eyes, 3/4" heart wattle)

TIP: Cut a White 3½" circle for body.

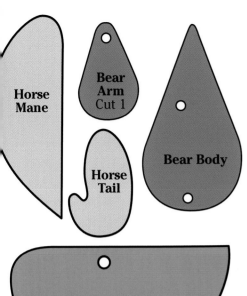

Horse Mane

Bear Arm Cut 1

Horse Tail

Bear Body

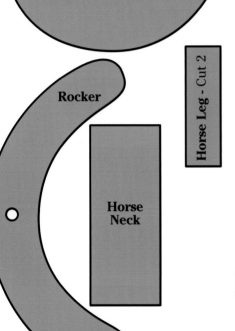

Horse Body

Rocker

Horse Leg - Cut 2

Horse Neck

Rocking horses, teddy bears, flags and a kid dressed in red, white and blue… American symbols all.

All American Kid

Design Originals 'Old Glory Flags on Blue' and 'Patriotic Flag' paper • Cardstock (Metallic Gold, Deep Red, White, Black, Brown, Tan parchment) • My Minds Eye title border • 3 Tan eyelets • Black pen • Corkscrew scissors • Circle punches (1/8" eyes and nose, 1/4" bear ears, 5/16" bear ears and tail, 5/8" spinner base, 1" bear head) • Heart punches (7/16" bear muzzle and horse ears, 1 1/4" bear legs and arms, 2" bear body and horse head)

TIP: Cut a 5/8" circle as a spinner base for the rocking horse.

A teddy bear and a horse invite you to rock into a party.

Party Invitation & Envelope

'Red Dot' paper • Cardstock (Royal Blue, Deep Red, Black, Brown, Tan parchment) • 1/2" Red letter stickers • 3 Tan eyelets • Black pen • Jumbo Scallop and Deckle scissors • Circle punches (1/8" eyes and nose, 1/4" bear ears, 5/16" bear ears and tail, 5/8" spinner base, 1" bear head) • Heart punches (7/16" bear muzzle and horse ears, 1 1/4" bear legs and arms, 2" bear body and horse head)

See envelope pattern on page 8.

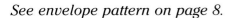

Pinwheels are magic! Every child remembers the spinning, whirling blur of pretty colors.

Pinwheel

Design Originals paper ('Pink stripe', 'Blue dot', 'Rose heart') • Cardstock (Rose, Baby Blue, Tan fleck) • ⅝" Baby Blue letter stickers • Blue eyelet • Seagull and Stamp scissors • Circle punches (¾" pinwheel center, 1¼" spinner base)

TIP: Fold pinwheel corners to center and glue. Glue small circle to center matching ⅛" holes. Place spinner base on back of pinwheel but do not glue. Set eyelet through center. Glue base to page.

A jolly little snowman brings you shovels full of Christmas cheer to brighten your day!

Snowman Card & Envelope

Design Originals 'Pine Tree Forest 'paper • Cardstock (Teal, Tan, White, Black) • ⁷⁄₁₆" White letter stickers • 2 White eyelets • Black and Orange pens • Deckle scissors • Circle punches (1" head and scarf, 1¼" upper body, 2" lower body)

See envelope pattern on page 8.

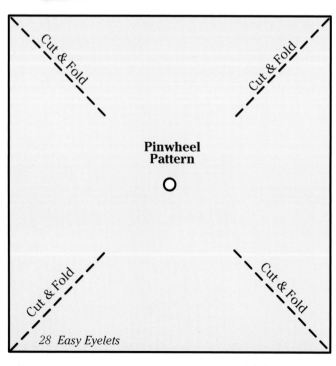

Pinwheel Pattern

○

Cut & Fold
Cut & Fold
Cut & Fold
Cut & Fold

Poseable Shapes for Clever Pages All Year Long!

Pose a snowman on a winter wonderland page covered with forest beauty and icy snowflakes.

Snowman

Design Originals Pine Tree Forest paper • Cardstock (Dark Green, Blue, White, Black, Tan) • ⅝" White letter stickers • 2 White eyelets • Black and Orange pens • Deckle scissors • 1¼" snowflake punch • Circle punches (1" head and scarf, 1¼" upper body, 2" lower body)

Spin the Pinwheel and Pose the Snowman's Arms to Change the Scene! All made possible with Easy Eyelets!

Top Hat

Shovel

Hatband

Top Hat

Face Pattern

Scarf

Scarf

Shovel Stick

Snowman Body

Shovel Handle

Snowman Arm
Cut 2

Tahoe

Poseable Shapes
Twist, Turn, Spin, Rock and Move!

TWINS

Andrew & Thomas

Move the Animal Ark, Elephant Trunk and Giraffe Head to Change their Poses!

Giraffe Horn
Cut 2 Each

Giraffe Head

Giraffe Mane - Cut Slits every 1/8" for Fringe
Glue Here

Giraffe Neck

Elephant Trunk

Elephant Head

Elephant Ear
Cut 2

Monkey Face

Lion Head

Giraffe Spot
Cut 7

Ark Roof

Ark

Animal Ark

Twins are double the trouble and double the joy, which makes for an ark full of fun and affection.

Animal Ark

Design Originals 'Water and Swirls' paper • Cardstock (Dark Teal, Deep Red, Yellow, Brown, Light Gold, Dark Gold, Black, Gray, Pink, White, Rust fleck) • Eyelets (Silver, Blue, Light Blue) • ½" and ¾" Red letter stickers • Black pen • Deckle scissors • Heart punches (7/16" giraffe ears, 7/8" ark trim, 1¼" elephant ears, 1¾" elephant ears, 2" giraffe head) • Circle punches (⅛" eyes and monkey nose, ¼" giraffe horn, monkey eyes and lion nose, 5/16" monkey hands and lion ears, ½" lion muzzle and hands, ¾" monkey head and face, 1" monkey body, 1¼" lion head, 1½" lion mane, 1⅝" elephant face, 2" spinner base) • Punches (⅝" spiral monkey tail, ⅝" sun lion mane, ⅝" egg giraffe spots)

Poseable Shapes

Eyelets make it possible to have poseable characters. Just set the eyelets a little tighter than you would for moveable pieces.

1. Punch and cut all pattern pieces. Punch ⅛" holes as marked. If design calls for spinner base, cut required circle, punch ⅛" hole in center and attach to back of the pattern piece with an eyelet.

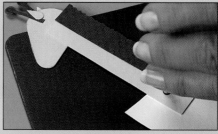

2. Match ⅛" holes and join design pieces with eyelets using an eyelet tool and hammer. For characters to hold pose, eyelet must be set firmly.

3. After eyelets are set, glue remaining pattern pieces together.

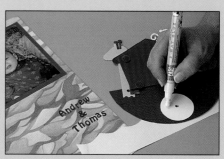

4. Glue stationary sections of completed design to album page. Moveable parts should be free and have room to move properly.

Swinger Flaps
Bring Photos Out of Hiding!

These boots are made for riding. Add a special friend and a faithful horse for the best in the west memories.

Best in the West
Design Originals 'Stepping Stones' paper • Cardstock (Rust, Moss Green, Tan parchment) • Silver eyelet • 5 Silver star nail heads • Black pen • Zig Zag scissors
TIP: Print sign on computer.
Tip: Cut sign from Tan parchment 4⅛" x 2½", sign post ½" x 2¾".

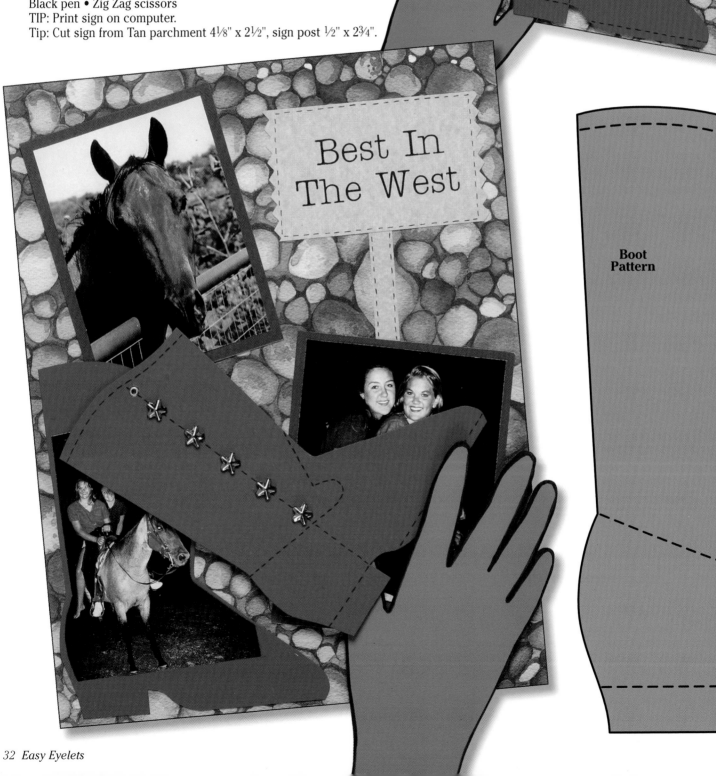

Best In The West

Boot Pattern

Move the Boot and Flower Flaps
to Reveal Great Photos!

Flower Pattern
Cut 8

Easter memories bloom on a page filled with the soft colors of of a wonderful spring day!

Happy Easter
Karen Foster Designs 'Peacock stripe' paper • Cardstock (Lavender, Purple, Pale Green, Yellow) • 'Easter' die cut • 4 Purple eyelets • Scallop scissors • Punches (1¼" circle photos, ¼" flower centers, 1" sun flower centers, 2" flower, 1" birch leaf)
Tip: Cut Pale Green ¼" wide flower stems, 2 at 2", 1 at 3½", 1 at 5" long.

Hang a row of Holiday ornaments that swing and twist to reveal bright smiling faces.

Christmas Ornaments
Design Originals 'Green Holly' paper • Cardstock (Red & White dot, Green, Deep Red, Metallic Silver) • Red 'Merry Christmas' die cut • 4 Silver eyelets • Stamp and Corkscrew scissors • Punches (¼" star, ⅜" heart, ¼" flower, ½" square ornament cap) • Circle punches (⅛" ornament trim, ¼" ornament hanger hole, ⁵⁄₁₆" ornament hanger, 1½" photo, 1⅝" photo backing, 2" ornaments)
Tip: Cut a Red & White dot strip ⅞" x 12".

Move the Ornament Flaps to Reveal Your Photos or a Hidden Message!

A Merry Christmas ornament hangs from a perky bow and brings cheery holiday wishes.

Christmas Ornament Card & Envelope
Design Originals 'Green Holly' paper • Cardstock (Green, Pale Green parchment, Red & White dot, Deep Red, Metallic Silver) • Silver eyelet • Stamp and Corkscrew scissors • ⅝" star punch • Heart punches (½" bow, 1¼" bow) • Circle punches (⁵⁄₁₆" for ornament hanger hole, ½" ornament hanger and bow center, 2⅝" ornament message, 3" ornament)
See envelope pattern on page 8.

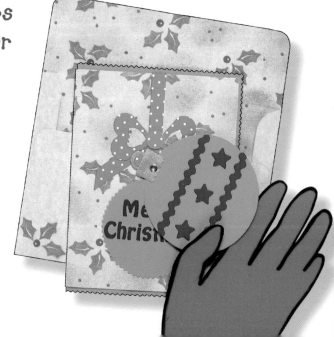